Emma & Egor

Signing Exact English

Emma

Eli

Egor

This Book is dedicated to Alexandra:

Thank you for being my ongoing inspiration in creating a **Signing Exact English** educational program that will positively impact the education and development of ALL children.

Copyright © 2018 by Stacy L. Eldred

This story and the characters of Emma and Egor are based on the ideas of Stacy L. Eldred.
Illustrations created by Lucía Benito

The characters, Emma and Egor, are trademarked by Stacy Eldred
Illustrations - Copyright © 2018 by Stacy Eldred

All rights reserved. No part of this book may be reproduced, transmitted, or stored in an information retrieval system in any form or by any means, graphic, electronic, or mechanical, including photocopying, taping and recording, without prior written permission from Stacy L. Eldred.

Visit our website at: **www.emmaandegor.com**

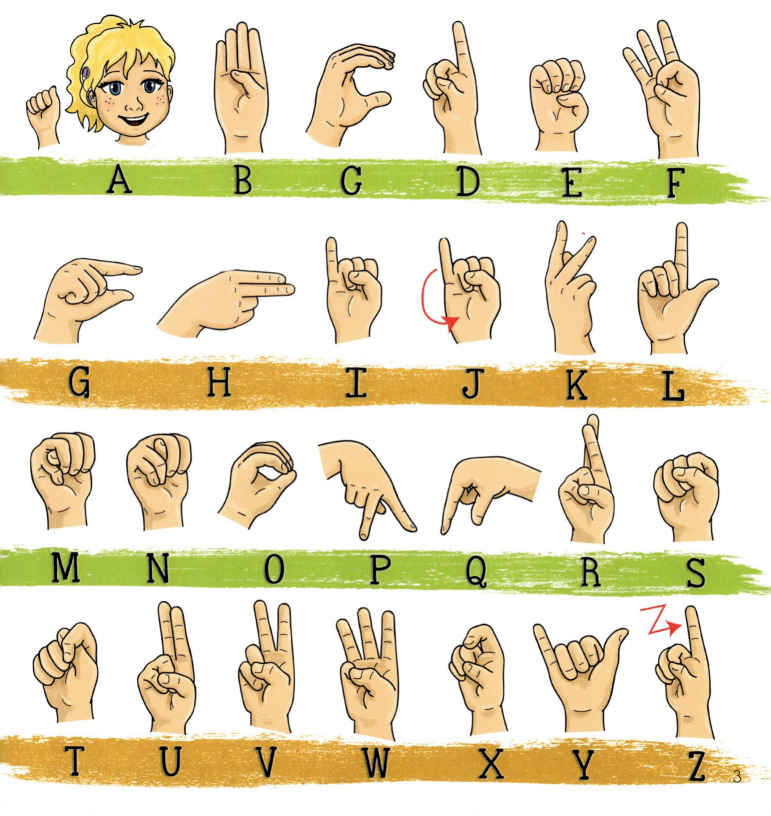

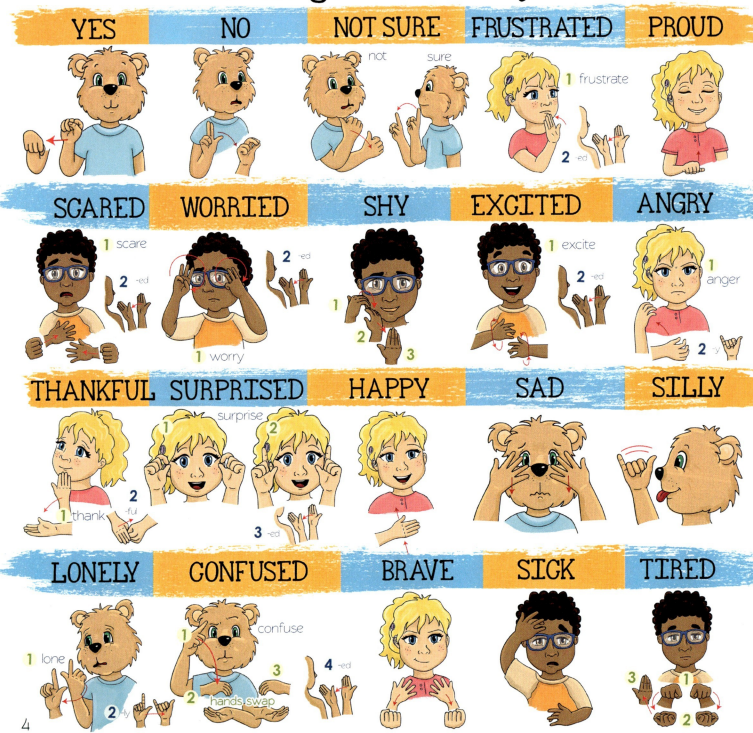

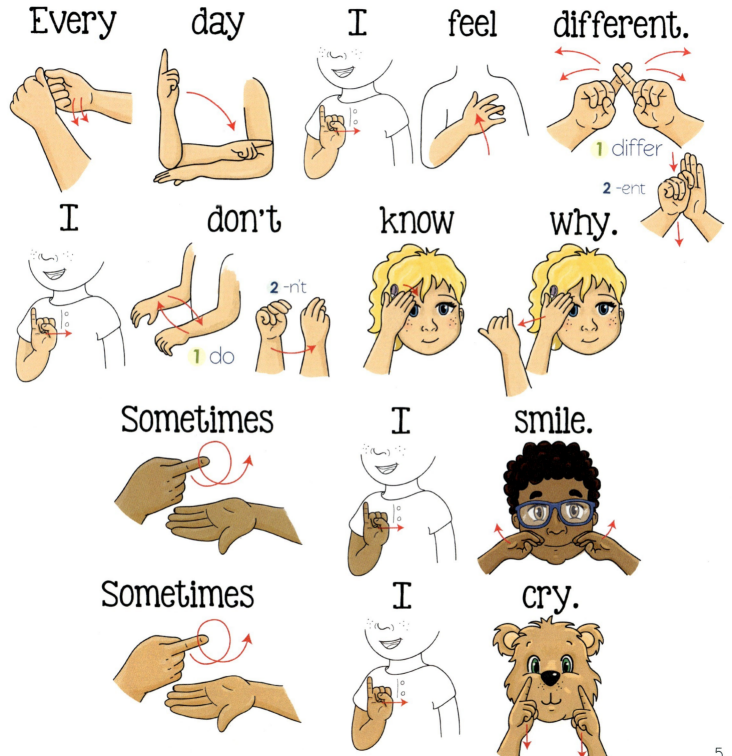

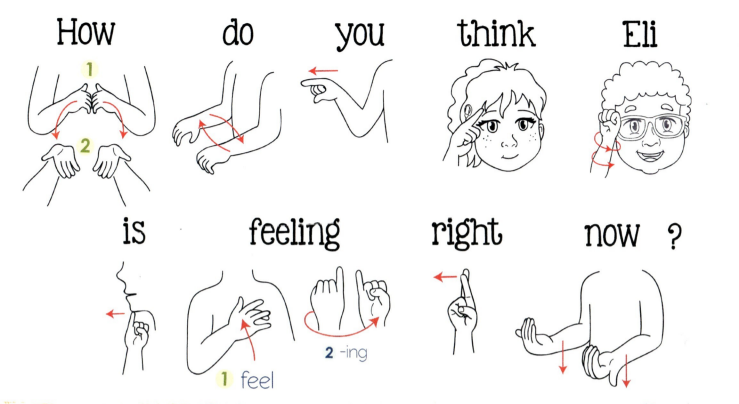

How do you think Eli is feeling right now?

WORRIED SCARED EXCITED SHY

Do you think they are happy to be friends?

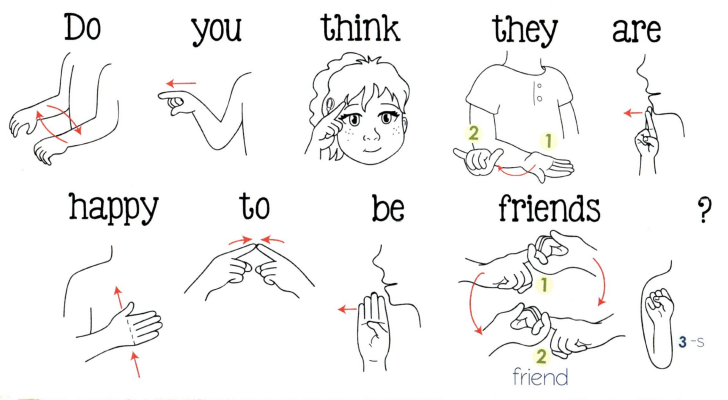

YES | NO | NOT SURE

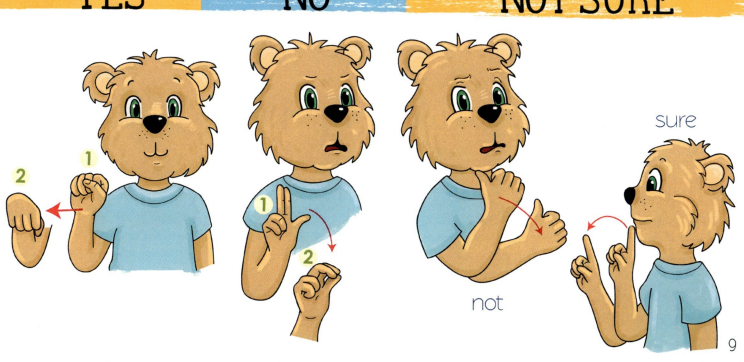

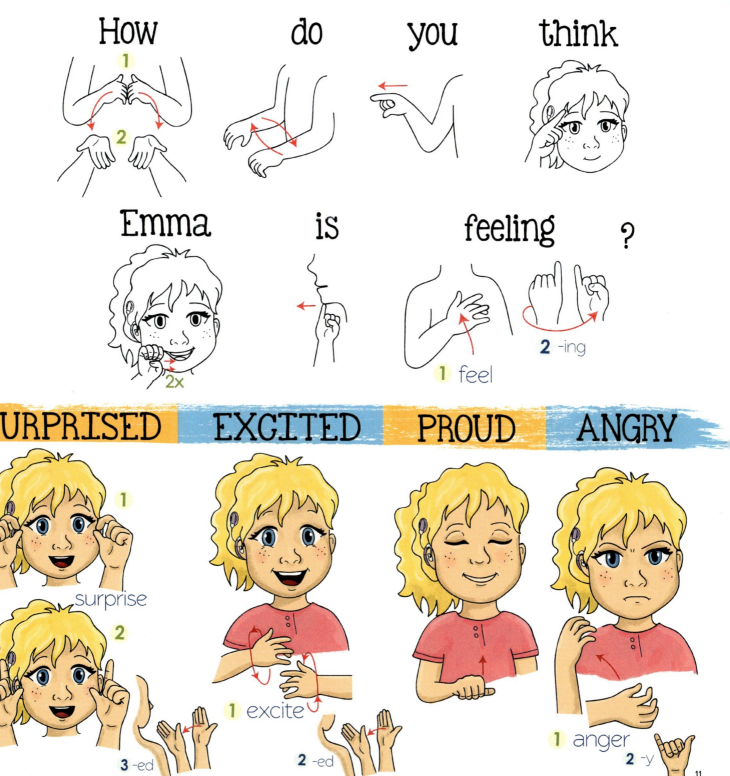

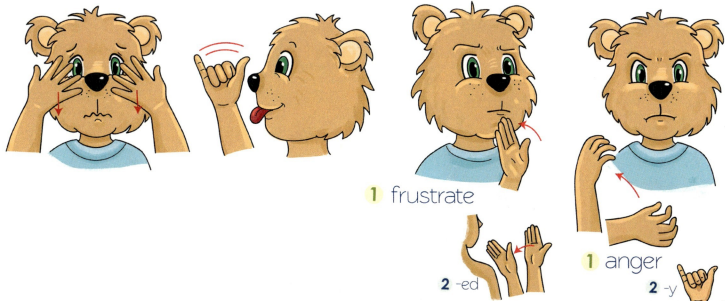

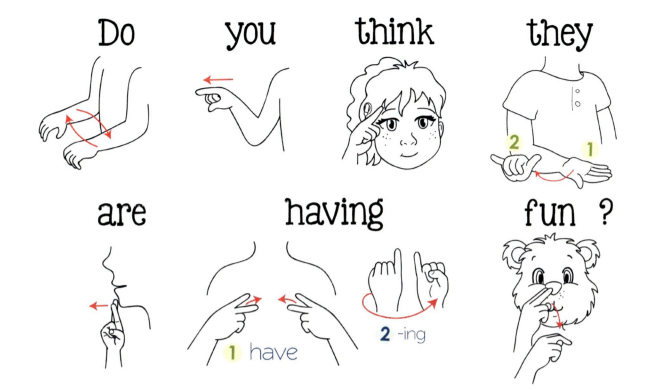

Do you think they are having fun?

YES | NO | NOT SURE

How do you think Emma

feels right now ?

BRAVE   SCARED   WORRIED   HAPPY

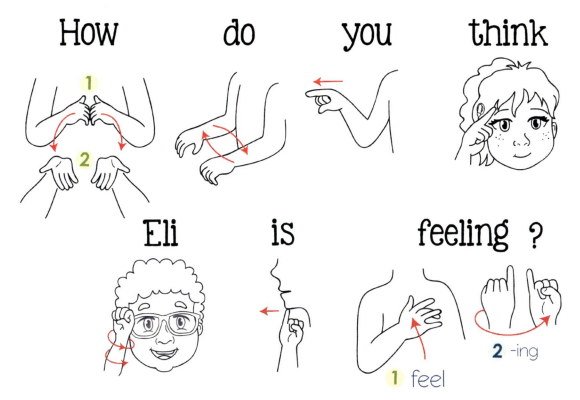

How is Egor

feeling?

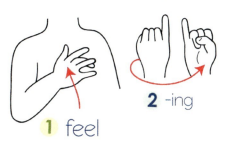

SILLY	TIRED	CONFUSED	SAD

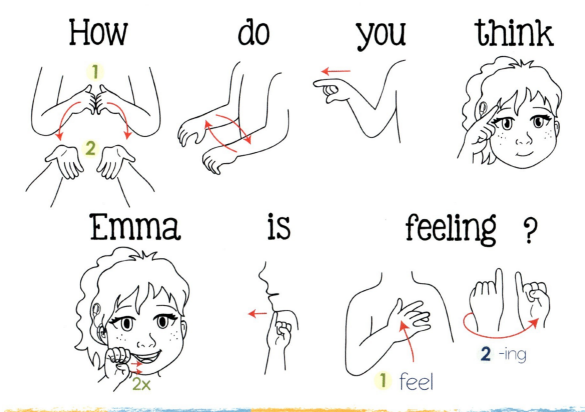
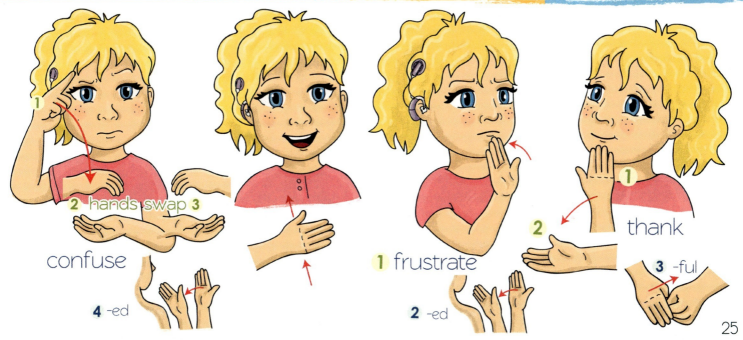

The End

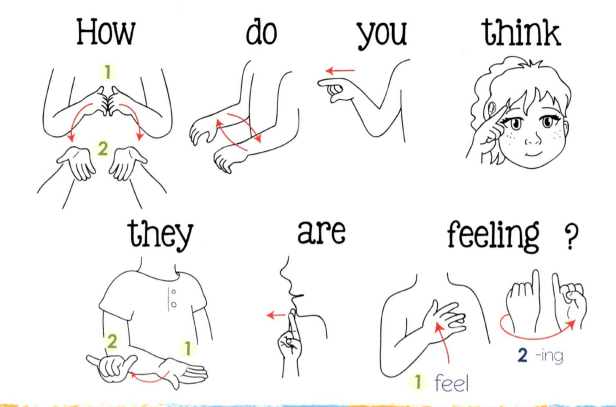

How do you think they are feeling?

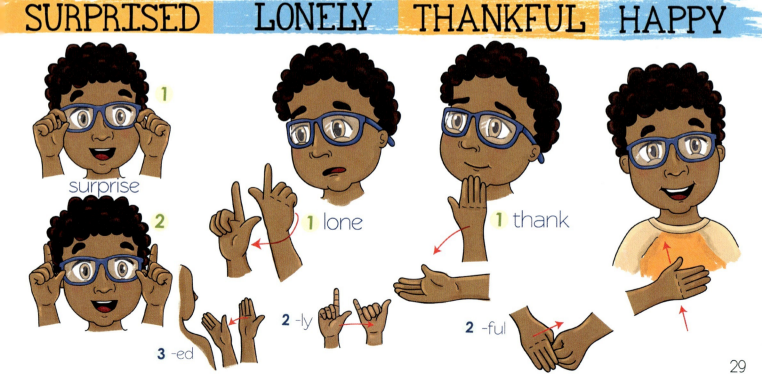

SURPRISED | LONELY | THANKFUL | HAPPY

About the Author

Stacy Eldred searched for years to find **resource books** and **teaching tutorials** for her **Deaf/Hard of Hearing** daughter. After teaching sign language to toddlers and preschoolers for over 10 years, she decided it was time to create a fun, easy, instructive and interactive way for teachers and parents to teach SEE (Signing Exact English) to hearing and non-hearing children. Thus Emma and Egor were born.

Stacy resides in Northern Virginia and had been developing her sign language skills for 21 years. Her passion is educating and nurturing the minds of children all over the world. It is her goal to reach as many people as possible through Emma and Egor.

About the Illustrator

Lucía Benito was born in Buenos Aires, Argentina, and has been drawing ever since she can remember. She has illustrated many children's books, as well as material for raising public awareness on environmental and social issues.

She considers herself blessed to be able to work at something she loves and in which she excels. In her own words:

"I truly believe that the greatest joy of being a graphic artist is to witness the happiness of the writer when they see their written words turn into images that had only existed in their imagination."

You can see more of her work at: www.tuolvidastodo.com

Made in the USA
Middletown, DE
27 October 2022

13593960R00018